Time of Fire

© Harry Laing 2023

Also by Harry Laing

> *Thirst* (Phoenix Press, 1993)
> *Backbone* (Bunda Press, 2010)
> *unsettled* (Walleah Press, 2021)

for children

> *Shoctopus* (Bunda Press, 2015)
> *MoonFish* (Ford Street, 2019)
> *RapperBee* (Ford Street, 2021)

This book is copyright. Apart from any fair dealing for the purposes of study and research, criticism, review, or as otherwise permitted under the copyright Act, no part may be reproduced in any manner without first gaining written permission from the author.

ISBN: 978-0-9804350-3-0
Bunda Press
PO Box 257
Braidwood
NSW 2622

Cover design, internal layout and set in Sabon 10.5/15 by Ingeborg Hansen
Cover photo by Harry Laing
Printed by Ingram Spark, Melbourne

BUNDA PRESS

TIME OF FIRE

Harry Laing

To Nicola

and

to Braidwood

Before

nothing was written
though some prophesied it was coming

neverbeendrier   neverbeen

offthecharts   notsincewhenever

nothing was written   not yet
the prophesiers held up their rain gauges
neveremptied   neverdrier

nothing was written not yet

except it was being written in the body
being written underfoot
day followed dry
followed day
followed dry lightning

dryknowing

hotdrywindofknowing

gutterclearknowing

words kicked away by the wind

because you can't remember can you

dry it was so dry
there's no way to remember how
sucked-in it was
the hollowness of the land
the hollow sound of walking
the ground of no-colour
not yellow not grey not moisture
not a vestige
the forest floor imploring
the straining of plants and trees
things were cracking inside
the stress was pitiful palpable
living things under such pressure
gathered into the smallest shapes
of the driest ever

no it was drier

signs and omens

rainforest burns
rainforest burns in winter

no denying the omens
no staring down the drought
the only defiance to keep living
everything else had dried up
what else was there to do

so we left and headed away
like we could shore up normality
was it defiance or denial or just living
leaving the signs and omens behind

and only much later hear how
one Monday night end of November
dry lightning speared North Black Range
and the person who saw it
knew that moment for what it was

knew they were in for it

the next day he was up there
second truck on the scene
couldn't find enough water
no water for the fire now with the name
North Black Range
moving east   head   flank   front
each day took a bigger chunk

he replays it again in his mind
first the forks go in
then the juddering the foreboding
he was second truck on the scene

so he replays it again
the forks go in the range lights up
always back to the beginning
those two huge forks
in for it we're in

everyone knows how it ran
          all the way to Braidwood
                    and it runs on in the head of this man

because he couldn't stop it

it continues expanding in his mind
over and over again
and he's helpless to do a damn thing

remember
the café in Maryborough   Victoria
when fire barged in the door
scorched the phone
entered the body by proxy

remember the phone calls
hanging onto the voice of a friend
as some kind of anchor
as she described air-tankers   fire outrunning trucks

remember reading a fire-map
in the wrong state
trying to make sense of the *finger of doom*
aimed at Reidsdale   *our place*

there was nothing we could do   remember
so we kept heading away
(in retrospect
treacherous)

travelling back we had miles of it
country untainted by smoke
and no idea how precious it was

then the first glimpse of home-country

and rearing over it
that hideous tower of lurch and scare
pyro-cloud
even from Yass it was massive
and you said *no*
not going there

and I thought fair enough
and we trembled accordingly
at the size of that pillar
as if we were nothing
and it wanted everything
we were fuel
even from that distance
we were fuel

entering its lands
the fear had started in earnest

no   you were not going there
not the dog either

Canberra
yes stay there   you and the dog
but I couldn't stay
the urge to get home
possessed by a force
I'd never felt before
like I didn't own my life
something else did
the gut-twisting alarm
as I gunned the car
racing for I didn't know what
fear lodged in the body
shaking the fabric
the fire-hold   that fear-grip
nothing I looked at was safe

past Bungendore
all landmarks gone
smoke pulled down low
hiding the slopes

how wrong it felt

fire lurking up in the range
a beast of unknown size
the emptiness of the highway
like I was the only car
heading into country silenced by smoke
the grey of it   the foreboding

the emptiness of the highway

going in
going under

at the fire station in Braidwood
the truck revved up in panic
and two firies yelling
are you getting on?

*because it's coming
coming to our country now*

I dithered I said no
bottled it
said *I have to check the house
need to check*

I couldn't hop up
put on the yellow gear
not yet
instead slunk away

to our place

Fire

that's where it'll come from
the north or the west

the mantra we used to repeat
demonstrating   arms wide
where the fire would come from

the north
sweeping through ninety degrees
to the west

paddocks in open agreement
the protection of two roads
the fire would have to leap them

it'll come from the north or the west

nobody told the Currowan Fire
born to the same lightning strikes
as North Black Range

the Currowan Fire
halfway to the coast
no conceivable threat

about to vault the escarpment
and come from the east

it'll never get over
  not the escarpment
there's a fair way to go
  they'll hold it on the Clyde
Government Bend
  plenty of trucks there
it's already beyond that
  spots on the escarpment
choppers can't fly
  too much smoke   too windy
keeps beating them
  easterlies
fire driven by south easterlies
  keeps spotting
keeps running
  up and over
it won't get into Monga
  can it get into Monga?
no way
  it's into Monga
the top end
  Woodleigh Fire Trail they'll hold it
plenty of resources
  dozers making lines
they'll hold it on the highway

having been a firie
for twenty years
back-of-the-truck ignorant
nursing a quiet hatred of outlets valves relays
flow rates all the lingo
still no idea how to work the radio
I got the call

found myself
wedged in the Cat 9 with the Captain
patrolling the highway
bits of black leaf drifting down   red leaf
shit this ember's live   his words
as the spot fires broke out over the road

competent or not
you get bounced around like a toy over tussock
and you do it
you get the hose on the spots
you put the bastards out

and you keep doing it
climbing into one truck or another
digging in   losing often
gaining just enough confidence
developing the fire-bones
to look the thing in the eye

days rolled by   days blurred
days lifted by a touch of exhilaration
discovering another save
house standing   garden smouldering
firies having just been in
and done the business
before hurrying on

I kept you in the phone-loop
told you how it was getting personal
this fire   as it moved into Monga
how I'd break myself to keep it out

you there in Canberra   hanging in
hearing the ebb and flow of my fear
my admiration for those firies
my despair for the creatures

I needed your voice   strong and clear
that reassurance

I hung on for it

the 12th the 25th the Friday or Monday
doesn't matter   leapt the King's Highway
we heard heavy plant over the radio
all units   get here real quick

the spot-fires had dropped in
horrible flowering
one there   another   there
it was gone
we raced around them and it was no good
ground too rough
flame taking hold   seizing
gathering
            vaulting the slope at speed
flame-height seven metres
                      we were told
it was gone
        we could see
                      the plume going up
that hideous dirty white climbing into the sky
                          pyro-cloud a kilometre high
the first giant bite into Monga
as the fire raced to the Northern Fire Trail
you knew it wouldn't stop
not for all the effort in the world
for all the backburning for all the strenuous hope
for all the rake hoes
                  and all the useless work
it was relentless let me tell you

heatblack
heartblack
lackheart
blackheat
blackedheart
blackwind
heatwind
burntair
rippedwhere
racedthrough
razedhill
dazednew
blackedout
smokeheld
burntworld

all day on the truck
carrying a day's exhaustion into the night-smoke
and a powerful need to be home

back to the house gone up in the mind's eye
how many times already
needing the house to tell me

junction and left and up and gate　turn
and it could be gone
can't be gone
but it could be gone

last corner just where belief is wafer thin
under the smoke pall that sucks everything dry

house

standing firm enough though weary
smudged　　jaded　　but standing

shrike thrushes still calling
keeping it all going
ribbon gums east and west

my head against the verandah post
my heart in that timber

house I'm holding against the fire

house

the sit of it
the risk in it
the bones of it
the hold of it

the life in it
the quiet of it
the threat to it
the set of it

to run from it
or stay with it
the thought of it
the thought of it
the thought of it

house

telling anyone in yellows
our place   defendable?
what do you reckon?

captains and deputies
firies in trucks far away
I was shameless
my claw on their arm   in their ear

that's our place
right on the edge
what would you do?

before it was offered
I took any help
no time for politeness
timber house in the worst place
what wouldn't I do
who wouldn't I grab

I was shameless

jumped the
            didn't you hear
containment line
            every time
where was the line
            doesn't matter
jump that one and the one after
            all that work
and they get jumped
            make your own line   make it here
break your back for the line
            down to the dirt do it right
use a rake hoe   scrape   doze it in
            doesn't matter
day or night it'll be jumped
            didn't you hear
jumped
            the
                        line
every bloody time

there was a roadblock at the end of the world
and it was always night
and the cars rolled up
and the smoke came down on the roadblock
and the lights flashed and the heart
slumped as if it hadn't slumped enough
and there was Jen at the roadblock
who stood in the middle of the smoke day and night
and she came to the car window
and listened like no-one else
how creatures were being turned to ash
and the desperate birds had nowhere to go
she listened and you loaded it on
but her shoulders were broad
and she lifted the weight off yours
and you left a little heartened just a fraction
taking that next stretch of the night
and there was no thrill
there was nothing exciting about any of it
not the flashing this or that
or the throbbing blades not the choppers
anyway there was a roadblock at the end of the world
and I kept drawing up to it dog-weary
and it was always night and I won't forget
the way she stood there
the way she heard me
heard us all
in the time of fire

morning or evening in the shed
hard to know which   a dismal briefing
maps featuring the fire's paw prints hatched in grey
yet more country snatched

next thing it was night and exhaustion
those miraculous hot dinners
at whatever o'clock
women handing out food
with a cheerfulness you didn't feel

the surge of silent relief
when you heard a friend's place
was still standing

but then the two firies in unison
chanting like some bloody Greek chorus

it's coming to your house
haven't you realised?
it's coming to everyone's house

and you begged them to unsay it

fire
the taker
the train the freight the coming
the break the spots the running
the plume the paw the pump the puff the char the more
the more the running the towers of smoke
the running the pall the smoke
the smoke the forest the paddock the day the week the lot

taken

off the truck

you'll need to look after your place

(if you can)

people   neighbours   connection
like I've never felt
ask anything   clearing   carting
checking   it would be done
and what you didn't ask for
hoses   rakes   water containers
would be there

this bond deep and unspoken
not mystical   visceral
you'd be panicking   text or ring
they'd come they'd work they'd reassure
not once   not once did anyone not come
there was no edge to this spirit

and I've never felt such
care   there were no barriers
the more the fire took
the more this feeling took hold
though no-one would admit it

say it

it was love

metallic alarm in edgy air
squealing tracks
the *chunk chunk chunk*
of dozers arriving

two machines at the gate
a grave-looking team   father and son
come to clear a line

and they did it carefully
more dirt-surgeons than anything
chunk chunk chunk
one behind the other
leader cutting
the follower heaping up
blackwoods were downed   yes
but the relief of bare dirt was a panacea
that defiance of mineral earth
something to stand behind

chunk chunk chunk

on they came
made side-circles round the huts and the tanks
then down to the dam and through the fence
and yes it was raw
but it was all you could do

chunk chunk chunk
off they trundled

the line ran the length of Reidsdale
this side of the forest
and now that fences were cut
one place flowed into another
bringing the vehicles in
locals seized by the need to check   affirm   exhort
or just shoot through
it was comforting though odd
like strangers wandering through your house
but with good intentions
it was freedom in dangerous times
the end of boundaries for now
a flowering of neighbourliness
a line drawn against the fire's relentlessness

the strange things people did
strung between one day and the next
forgetting their own names
as fire swallowed localities
moved always a little closer
broke yet another line

and no wonder some folk pulled up at road junctions
and hurled prophecy down from truck windows
how the whole lot was going up *all of it*
every stick from here to Victoria

and you listened because you had to hear the worst
hoping it wasn't true knowing it was

and next thing
spotfires of suspicion and outrage
some nonsense about water
fire speaking its guttural rubbish
and you   gusting hard and angry
driving the car way too fast
smacking the wheel

feeling you could go up that easy

fire-waiting
the dry mouth of waiting
sweating on something unseen

the one thing coming
that keeps you raking and raking
lifting and heaving
years of bark   tinder   ribbons
sticks   leaves   all this stuff
should have been shifted
heaving and hauling and loading
and carting

checking gutters again
sweeping dead leaves
ground beyond brown
wind's evil intent
the whole lot could go up for looking
thirty eight thirty nine the smoke's done your brain
the heat's the fire speaking
freaking you out

wanting it here wanting it over
wanting it never
texting and waiting
phone pinging
someone's on their way
to join you in waiting
join you in heaving and hauling
no-one saying much

what's coming
will say it all

your wooden bubble   octagon
eye above the glade
timber and glass
first thing the fire would find

we both agreed   no chance

we'd done the calculation
wind divided by timber plus position
equals inevitability

friends had pulled out all the under-grass and bracken
a dirt line had been dozed

now it was on its own

not far away
but where?
up the top of Tudor Valley Road
to the north then   or was it more east
smoke the rumour
panic the fact

couldn't work out where it was

it it it
in the gut
the near of **it** the where of **it**
the beginning the no end of **it**

the one thing not waiting

was **it**

at the junction

roared   the neighbours said

up on the ridge
it was roaring
it roared all night

like what?   wind   train   jet?
insane with itself it roared
sucking the life out of Monga
up and down the ridge it roared
taking forest south and east
taking more

and this morning
was back to menacing
jinxing round puffing up
impossible to tell where

and when I got to the house
I couldn't believe how delicately
the black leaves were scattered on the steps

at the house
on my own
this the day
north west wind
hot as fuck
behind the line
trailer and tank
couldn't stand still
walking that nerve-edge
checking on twisted
dirtymad smoke
up behind
constantly thinking
it's coming in
it's coming in
it's coming in
coming now
coming now
coming in
in
in
in

where?

had to find it

in the drum of the afternoon
in the dry of the yellowness
in the heat of the waiting

to find it
just to know

where it was

like walking
over powdered glass
pushed by adrenalin
walking fast
up the slope of alone
every step wrong
past my hut   past yours
past the tank

mouth dry as dirt
like the fire could just erupt

the way everything tensed
like it knew

up over Doug's track I could hear it
must be a little further
back of the gully   there

live

the line of it   ragged orange line
working down the far side

the intent
the need to hurt
the lure the leer the glare
the raw the maw
the noise the working away
the smoke
no attempt to disguise itself

unstoppable riveting orange

that firemouth

(firemouth speaking)

you

you and me

watch

no-one else

watch me take

personal

this is yours

it belongs

ran back

alone

there were seven   a cavalcade
seven utes on the drive
I'd never asked
the afternoon's mouth wide open
mine too
mozzies burning up the drive
in answer to panic and unspoken prayer
the rightness the timing
exquisite   out of the blue
abandonment's answer

maybe they'd clocked the smoke
seen it swinging about
I'd never asked
they were here
hopping down
mostly strangers   some faces I knew
as they took up positions

just as you're chewing yourself up
the bodies arrive

beautiful people beautiful water tanks
all unbidden

and Duncan and Mish
plied water over the wooden sides of the octagon for an hour
as if the fire would pay the slightest attention

the beast lurking off
wouldn't come in
everyone left

to get some sleep

10pm
five minutes lying down
felt all wrong
opened my eyes
and the sky was orange

pure dread   that leer
threat of that hideous sky
I ran out
certain of fire

rang triple O
there was one truck left   somewhere
it came
a couple of sturdy women jumped out and agreed
the fire-beast was mad with itself
a little way back in the trees
the way it was gorging

they were cheerful
but a sky like that
back of your place

you don't forget

change of shift
first truck filled up from the house tank and left
the replacement arrived
two or three old blokes got out
carefully

unfussed by what they could see of the fire
decided where to burn from
(obvious)

and we all waited some more

time came
they lit up and *pouf*
the small basketed geebung
on the edge of the dirt line went up
like a magic trick

the firie was cranky

shit!
I was trying to save that

the way it came in the small hours

the way the wind pushed
the way the fire took what was given
ignored the glade
kept its head down

the way I kept my eyes open
the way we stared each other out

the way

we still had a house

and when the firie went for a look
treading his way through the burning scraps

he came back saying *the shack's still there*
chuckling with surprise

luck and the lack of it
how to keep track of it
wish me luck blackens it

take wind   the tack of it
some prayed for the back of it
so many were racked by it

the same wind no slack in it
saved us   the knack of it
luck lived there   a pack of it

fire sniffed the lack in it
came quiet   the tack of it
we had luck and a stack of it

morning or whatever it was
with fire trucks
folk hosing down trees
firies setting backburns
wind whipping things along

mozzies and others emptying their tanks
relief as wide as an exhausted sky
the smoking grief of the forest
and no letting up on the action
people bodies utes
everyone had a hose

like the hinges had loosened
anything could happen
I was stopped by two French filmmakers
and a camera
had I seen creatures running from the forest?
the fire was talking gibberish
I had no idea what I'd seen
or who they were

only later saw what I looked like
a mad smudged Lear
hair standing up
completely gone

sitting at the table
first time in twenty four hours
(no fire under the table)
and the edges of the forest secure
(so far as I knew)

in a state of numb
stupefied by the mug of tea
limbs and brain reeling

the wind   had it changed?
dragged myself out again
and yes   smoke
hitch trailer and tank

fire's taking the paddocks
careering across to Frank's
having another go on the forest edge
could run for the house
with a push from the south east

get the hose on   give it some
the grader's flying though the murk
cuts the fence puts the line in
RFS vehicle shoots up   wheels round
disappears back down the drive

you're just having a tea break
fire's taking your paddocks

the bastard

I drove out that evening
New Year's Eve supposedly
blackwoods and ribbon gums opposite the gate
burning enthusiastically
greeting or farewell
who knew

out though the gateway
gate lying there
one post a pile of charcoal
the other smouldering
and liberation to leave
with the house standing

so what if the gateposts were still burning
we were all unhinged

I can't remember
other than being clean

we were together in town
there were drinks
but I can't remember

something huge had happened

happy new year

New Year's Day
I wanted you to see
I needed you to witness
how our place survived
look   touch   believe

and I needed you to know
about the appetite of fire
and together this time
we hosed it
still creeping away
under the double-trunked blackwood

later that morning
having reclaimed the place
fire trucks came round
a grizzled captain wept with relief
to see the house standing
to see us

such were the times

After

silence
hurt silence

sound
of the stripped

charred quiet
the smell of it

silence

the dead in
the dead of

silence

ash bed
no markers

a dead glider
by the looks

humps and vertebrae
of the forest floor
revealed

counting the ancestor trees
some of the oldest
burnt out
come down

others standing
with a certain defiance

family flew over
soon as they could

we had no water
header tank smashed by a giant tree

hauling a small tank up the slope
plumbing it in

even that small act
putting water back
where it belonged

helped

any talk of stark beauty

red-gold leaves on black ground

even from family

couldn't hear it

huge snake-roots that had never been seen

and the other discoveries
the broken bottles at the base of the biggest trees
a hubcap   old tins   indecipherable metal

strange touch of the human

in burnt world

have you bought a lottery ticket? she asks
why?
you're the luckiest man in Braidwood

hearing it
from someone else's mouth
so it must be true
kind of a sudden glow
a shiny feeling in the middle of town
knowing fine that saving the place
had nothing to do with me
not really
it was the luck of the wind
the people who turned up
the worrying from afar

but I'll take it   the shine
take a minute's worth of glow

you're the luckiest man in Braidwood

sure

walking over ash bed
you didn't know whether it could live again
whether anything would return
nobody knew   nobody

and you looked and the ash bed looked back
and you didn't believe   not a word
was there anything
was there a pulse
was there a beginning
under that burnt deck
would anything come

and you waited not knowing
even learnt a little about not knowing
the floor was burnt the sky was burnt
the in-between was burnt
and nothing that skittered or slithered
had survived

first wombat
maybe five days in
you saw it

very much alive
emerging out of the ravaged
face and fur intact
no trace of fire on him or her

you communed with this survivor
from the slope-city of wombats

laid out carrots   sweet potato

something took them
bower birds probably

but the wombat kept appearing

ready to talk

a week after
I headed up through the buckled deadscape
to the top of Monga

that pinkwood grove
most secret rainforest
held in the cleft under the mountain
had it survived?
(knowing it couldn't have)

up the Old Araluen Road
working over and around huge fallen silvertops
(how could anything have survived?)

then the approach
first glimpse of the rainforest curtain
some hope in that darker green

slipping down the blackened rocks
saluting the centuries-old brownbarrel sentinel
battered   alive   half what it was

then through the curtain   fire-thinned
to the offering of ancient quiet
hundred year old vines still twining

the giant pinkwoods upstanding

I was there
saved your place
came with the mozzies

good job   thanks   meant a lot

we were on the truck
got called away
otherwise would have
saved your place

supermarket   main drag   butchers
fire shed   you name it

saved your place
I was there   remember
yes   thanks again   great job

your place
I was there

cartons of beer for the saviours
a cheer for the saviours

evidence of fallen trees
but no sign of their bodies

distinct white-grey outlines
on dirt burnt red
neat piles of charcoal vertebrae

vestige and simulacrum

bodies vaporised
and rearranged

in the stun-scape in the burn-scape
in the black of so much dying
there were days of almost nothing
of the living there was nothing
but the falling   just a smatter
and a falling of the colour
of the dead leaves' silent scatter

there were days and days of waiting
days of walking trying something
in the silence of the shattered
fallen giants the smoking hollows
days of wispy smoke and smoulder

days of nothing doing
there were days and days of listening
flash of green   a fungus-fingering
and somewhere in the monochrome
treecreeper piping   so much feeling
surge of pleasure just one creature

after all the death and taking
you're so much closer to the living
there's a fierceness to the living
when you start again from nothing

and it could

    impossible to believe

it could

    could still rain

it did

    24mm

mid-January

    smell of wet ash

out on the truck
trundling down the edge of Monga
offering reassurance
which nobody needs
now that it's all burnt
the dice have been rolled
and most folk have winged it
for some too close
the relief on this still day
eating the sandwiches
taking the view in
fires to the south yes
no concern there
relief that it's over
relief with a dark edge
hard not to think
of the forest destroyed
the burnt body of forest

technically it was closed   the forest
danger of falling trees etc.
the word *danger*
laughable after the cataclysm

one or two strong souls
were putting out food and water
going deep into Monga   for the creatures
all praise for their efforts
I didn't want to go
couldn't bear to see

but some reckoning had to be made

and in we went   Alex and I
walked Boundary Fire Trail
to Milo Mountain and it was worse
it was better   no it was worse than we thought
it was ripped through
it was bombed in places
almost untouched in others

there's a photo at the top of Milo
Alex and the trig   its plastic top melted
a background of blasted alpine ash

and there wasn't much more to say
and seeing was better than imagining

so long waited for
so much to appease
this time for real

Feb 8 2020

as if it couldn't believe itself
this rain came battering with the force of need
with a pent up desperate too-lateness

crazed   the way it came
crazed glorious mad stuff
sluiced ash off the forest
left no surface unscoured

creeks   new ones
rushed past garden gates
black torrents over the paddock
ash   burnt bits   seed capsules
driven with fury
into the dam's dry eye
heaped a black island
a stash of burnt country in black water

taking it in   flush-happy
taking it deep
rain-salve for wounds and for rawness

the unwipeable grins
of *how much? how much?*

all of us filling up at last
for the first time in years
that sound   from deep inside
not hollow any more

our cups running over
we were drunk with it

the question of webs after rain
their poise

the dead blackwood festooned
with spider-eyes

what does it take to be upright
to remain standing after all that?

the webs shake their rain-beads
tremble with life

gossamer décor
some spidery meaning
to those black limbs

light through the forest
where it shouldn't be
like the sky has broken in
forest's bitten into
it hurts to see the frailty

before the fire
was constant shade
trees stepping forward with assurance
the endless forest body
unbroken canopy

now cracked with sky

and it was the treeferns
astonished us all

stripped to sticks
blackened verticals
no vestige of fern-tracery
all the green light gone
lifeless we thought

but they proved us wrong
came back from nothing
out of thin air
first a knuckle then a finger   unscrolled
uncurled an arm   many fern-arms
entire slopes re-lit with green crowns

they roared back
and made it look easy
shrugged off our doubts
pushed up and out   the muscle
deep in them
Gondwanan foreknowledge
fire-knowledge

we pointed at them
exclaimed at such insouciance   such defiance
we admired every frond

having imagined them such delicate creatures

so happy to be wrong

months after
having heard how fire-plundered it was
down there
the scale of it
having quietly put it off

first trip to the coast
dead trees everywhere
vistas of burnt-world

the revelation of rock a sort of nakedness
the rock-body of the land
something that shouldn't be seen

here it was   grey-bald   fur burnt off
awful to see how it was put together
valley and peak   hump and bluff

skeletal
          exposed

before
the place you can't go back to
before

the trees of *before*
and the forest of *before*
the former rhythm of unburnt trunks
buff   grey   cream
uplifts twists and angles

the once-veil of peppermint foliage
leaf litter
the rustle underfoot

carrying round *before*
in this new world that has no interest
and shrugs off any mention of

before
    before
        before

like something was right with the world after all
like someone had noticed

La Niña and her rainy gift
tipping out her Pacific skirts

month after month
dousing the memory of flame

so something was right with the world after all
justice was being done

and not one of us game
to say *slow down*

forest slopes where spring is moving
look past the standing dead silvertops
keep the eyes down
keep them low

look at the gang of orchids
spikes of blue   a riot of white
the seedling army
swarming

your looking speeds the growing

roadside number
offered at the gate
summons
little metal prayer
talisman for rescuers   fire trucks

everyone has one
ours is *blank blank bent four burnt nine*
pocked   cooked
a testament to that loudmouth fire
counting in its own language
took the gateposts and left our number

dangling

I lift it from the ash
cut its wire ties
leave it lying around
hoping it might enlighten me
blank blank bent four burnt nine

in walk the weeds
take the bare-dirt offer
swagger in like the bastard colonisers they are

fire-spawn
            junket of skank-stems
                                    gross leaves
on steroids

unnaturally green   ankle-clutchers
seed-spewers   rank blankets
the manic stems ooze when snapped
spring straight back
and smack you

curse the lot
heap   pile   make no headway
clear a small space a square metre maybe

to laughs from the weed army pissing themselves
puffed up with possession
knowing they are the inheritors

with visitors
repeating what happened
the same action in the same place in the same words
mantra and incantation
where it went what it did

necessary chant
on the rounds
pointing out where it came
where the backburn went in (2am)

where Duncan worked
back of those big brownbarrel
took his piece of bark and lit up
steered that little burn
like he'd done it all his life

where the grader line went
horseshoe round the house
the huge ribbon that should have gone up and didn't

clapping hands
in front of the unburnt trees
bringing in the gang-gangs
to reassure the place

repeating what happened and where
so it might not happen again

a year on   though nobody's counting
we are gathered
ready to be reminded

like burnt driftwood
we've been rolled around
and swept in here
to *Art on Fire*   the exhibition
carried by a swell-tide of emotion
no visible char on our hands
but look we carry it   the fire

we have never been so close
our bodies could be exchanged
we speak for each other
some weep

and it's not even us
it's something deeper
what these images and forms point to
what the walls vibrate with

the fire-scar that sings

I had to buy it
shiver of a thing

the photo that takes me apart
every time I look
the unholy way the fire
crests the escarpment at night
the raging beauty of it   necklace   horror

I have to look away
while it seizes the Budawang Range

have it propped on a bookcase
above eye level
still roaring
jewel   necklace   horror

shiver of a thing
I had to buy it

gang-gangs the long-living
long-loving couple
dipping and jinking
through the burnt heads

family
what are they thinking?
what do you say
to the pair sidling together
up a love-branch

having survived
having surveyed the ash
taken the blackened forms to heart
having no choice

I wish you hollows
I wish

crimsoncherryhead
creaking away   crooning to her
high up
catching the first sun

and the come again fungi
steady workers and sturdy believers
preaching from a perch on every toppled tree
the doctrine of new life
the fire that made it possible
charred trunks and fallen bodies their platform
where they spring from
miniature brackets of striped beige
orange peel wedges
and in the hollow of a giant brownbarrel
most secret gallery   a patch of moist jade sheen
neither moss nor algae
and the ruched lines of something fawn   repeating
design like a Victorian dress hem
so exquisitely stitched I can't believe what I'm seeing
the upsurge from every angle
every inch of ground
the hakea wattle already three metres
blackwood rampant   groves of adolescent trees
the sound of recovery
the deafening cheers of the fungi

even the dead trees
even the dead trees shift in the wind

animated by the game

tracing circles with stiffened tips
doing the best they can

the wind distributes itself
tender-heartedly
and it's touching to see the dead branches move
as if the branches remember the game

as if there's any difference
between dead and alive
bare and leafed

just a shift in the wind

above all the need to remember
smudge your fingers black
this dead tree needs touching
body head arms
prop yourself inside the hollow creature
and remember
despite the depth of the new green underfoot
the tangle of rain-sodden geranium
and the forest floor turned to sponge

remember

proof the world is fuel
these words are flammable
these firelines combustible

everywhere you look
is looking back with intent
saying *if not now when*

even rock   the optimist
that sanguine face
has been blacklisted   cracked open

and if rock is stirred
dirt is fuel
innocence is fuel
living is loaded

we are consumable

you   fire

don't want another whiff
not another puff from you

I wouldn't trust what I'd do
if you appeared on the horizon
and defaced that blue sky
with your come-again graffiti

I don't care to recognise your cue
that yellow look
as hills and slopes cure three years on
and even today's warmth has an edge

why don't you piss off   there's no name
and no place for you

not this season
not ever

how long
will the highest ridges
be gap-toothed
like broken combs

when will the silver grey highlights
criss-crossing the slopes
disappear

after a night of wind
flakes of charred bark on the road

old burnt skin blowing

and visible now   tree-muscle
breaking through   pale brown
show of strength

brownbarrel   peppermint

life

encountering those-who've-been-through-it

the fire-grip
metaphorical wrist-grab

the need that lies just under the surface
like something is keeping it warm
perhaps it burns

it sits in us
no   not sits   flickers
it glows

a conversation that blows back on itself
a necessary re-scattering of embers

a fire-grip that will only ever ease

in the telling

Notes

North Black Range Fire   started by lightning strike 26th November 2019 in the Great Dividing Range west of Braidwood.

finger of doom   a black-hatched area on the fire map where the North Black Range fire ran across the Cooma Road on 30th November.

Reidsdale   locality SE of Braidwood in the Southern Tablelands of NSW.

pyro-cloud   pyrocumulonimbus, a cloud that forms above a source of heat, such as wildfire. Many were created by the 2019/20 bushfires.

fire station in Braidwood (also referred to as **shed** or **fire shed**) Rural Fire Service NSW, Braidwood brigade.

Currowan Fire   started by a lightning strike on 26th November in Currowan State Forest which lies between the escarpment and the coast, east of Braidwood.

the Clyde   local name for the Kings Highway named after Clyde Mountain on the escarpment.

Government Bend   a steep hairpin bend on the same road.

Monga   Monga National Park, in particular the plateau section of tall wet forest with a western boundary to Reidsdale.

Woodleigh Fire Trail   a fire trail at the northern end of Monga NP.

Cat 9   a converted Toyota Landcruiser and smallest of the vehicles used by the NSW Rural Fire Service.

heavy plant   RFS captain or officer in charge of directing local building of containment lines.

Northern Fire Trail   a fire trail in Monga NP running due north from the Old Araluen road.

yellows   PPE (personal protective equipment) i.e. the heat-resistant clothing worn by firefighters.

containment line   a dirt line made by a bulldozer to prevent fire spreading across it. Also used as a secure edge from which to conduct a backburn.

roadblock   many local roads were blocked for the duration of the fires. These roadblocks were manned day and night and only bonafide locals allowed access to their particular locality.

women handing out food   the production of food i.e. lunches and hot dinners for firefighters in various of the fire sheds was a huge and brilliantly run operation.

your wooden bubble   Nicola Bowery's writing space

Tudor Valley Road   dirt road running north-south parallel to the western edge of Monga NP.

mozzies   unofficial firefighters known as *mosquitoes*. Every district/ locality had its quota of locals with utes loaded with 1000 litre water tanks, pumps and hoses. They were an invaluable part of the firefighting effort.

geebung   the shrub/ small tree *Persoonia linearis*, a common understorey species in Monga NP. And also the name of our property.

dead glider   greater glider, large gliding marsupial. Nocturnal and arboreal. Many were killed in the 2019/20 fires and as a result were listed as endangered by the Federal Government.

pinkwood grove   pinkwood, *Eucryphia moorei*, dominant tree species of cool-temperate rainforest of southeastern NSW. Some of the pinkwoods in Monga NP are thousands of years old and (mostly) survived the fires.

Old Araluen Road   fire trail in Monga NP that heads over Monga Mountain and joins the Kings Highway.

brownbarrel   *Eucalyptus fastigata*, dominant tall eucalypt of Monga NP.

huge fallen silvertops   *Eucalypus sieberi*, tall eucalypt growing on drier, stonier N/ NW facing aspects of Monga NP.

Boundary Fire Trail   fire trail in SE of Monga NP that follows part of the old State Forest boundary.

Milo Mountain   highest point in Monga National park, in southern portion.

alpine ash   *Eucalyptus delegatensis*, grows between 900m and 1450m altitude. Has no epicormic buds and hence is killed by severe fire.

grader line   dirt line that circled the house as a buffer/ protection against the fire.

Art on Fire   an exhibition featuring visual art and text mounted by the Braidwood Regional Arts Group in December 2020.

Budawang Range   part of the escarpment due east of Braidwood.

peppermint   *Eucalyptus radiata*. Common eucalypt in forests of SE Australia.

In addition to being a poet Harry Laing is a comic performer and children's author. He strongly believes poetry should be heard and is an energetic and dynamic reader of his work. For many years, together with his partner, poet Nicola Bowery, he has co-led the popular PoetryAlive weekend workshops. He also runs writing workshops in schools and regularly performs for hundreds of schoolchildren. Harry lives beside Monga National Park near Braidwood on the Southern Tablelands of NSW.

www.harrylaing.com.au

Acknowledgements:

Several of these poems were broadcast and recorded at the *Heart of The Storm* podcast launch in Braidwood, December 2022

Special thanks to Nicola Bowery for her editing skills and for her willingness to re-enter the fire forcefield.

www.ingramcontent.com/pod-product-compliance
Lightning Source LLC
Chambersburg PA
CBHW031426290426
44110CB00011B/536